LADYBIRD

Poems Of Personal Odyssey

SUBAH

INDIA • SINGAPORE • MALAYSIA

ISBN
Paperback 979-8-89363-390-0
Hardcase 979-8-89363-935-3

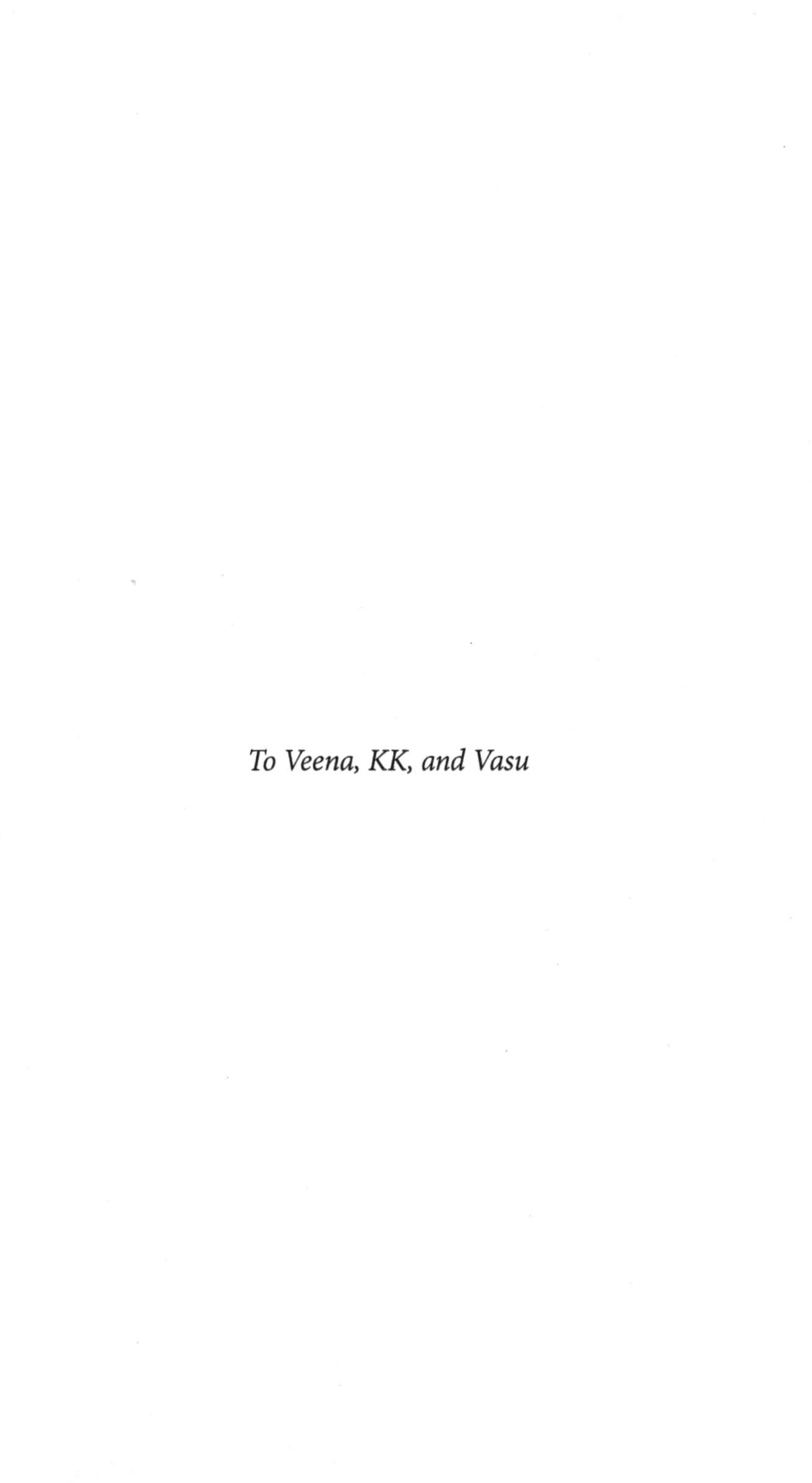

To Veena, KK, and Vasu

CONTENTS

1. Love's Evolution 2
2. Let Me Be 4
3. Melodies of Absence 6
4. Yearning for the Celestial 8
5. Where is my place? 10
6. Fractured Resolve 12
7. Awakening the Writer Within 14
8. Silent Reverberations 16
9. Mirage 18
10. Your sweet Albatross! 20
11. A Day of Liberation 22
12. Transient Blossoms 24
13. Shattered Trust 26
14. Unanswered Questions 28
15. Rainy Reverie 30
16. Roots of Anguish 32
17. A Shower of Solace 34
18. Freedom's Embrace 36
19. Flight of Resilience 38

20. Eternal Devotion 40

21. You were my Hero 42

22. Desert Blossom 44

23. Awakening 46

24. A Bittersweet Echo 48

25. Fragments of Sorrow 50

26. Not so Departed Love 52

27. A Dance of Truth 54

28. Nature's Lap 56

29. O' My Fragile Heart 58

30. Unbreakable Wings 60

31. The Fault in My Stars 62

32. Lost and Found 64

33. I am Nobody's Poetry 66

34. Swings were Cool 68

35. The Gaze 70

LOVE'S EVOLUTION

At fifteen, she harbored a dream,
Of love's sweet embrace, her soul's true mate
But time unfurled a different theme,
Love's not a paradise, nor fate's dictate

Things don't align as once she thought,
Soul mates aren't just those we've adored
They're protectors, healers, lessons taught,
Filling voids within, our spirits restored

No longer a mystery, he stands clear,
Her thoughts entwined, no longer mere
Love's evolution now draws near,
Unplanned, but timed, its essence sincere

This is how love's concept shifts and ranges,
Ever-evolving, as our lives rearrange

LET ME BE

On the set of dusk
I'm sluggish and tired,
Thriving for silence and calmness
In the darkness of the night
Hoping for some sleep

I see the stars and the moon
The vast sky and dark trees,
The hooting birds and crickets noise
Appreciating God's creation
Before I close my eyes

Embrace the cold winds until I get goose bumps
Thinking of my actions I have performed
That's when my memories haunt me,
And slowly, slowly
I lose my silent dreams

Sulking under the debris of thoughts
As I see a ray of hope,

I prophesize what I want to be
Not under the burden of bonds,
No more in denial, no loose ends
Let me be, I'm my strength

MELODIES OF ABSENCE

In my room of memories, nostalgia lingers,
Reminding me of the highs and lows,
Once bowed by sorrow, now standing tall,
Those tears shed, now mere echoes

Flashes of the past still haunt with anxiety,
Yet I sweat, I swoon, I endure the pain,
Swallowing the bitter pill of yesterday,
Seeking light amidst the shadows of disdain

Memories, they both strengthen and weaken,
Nightly sighs echo our moments lost,
Lost in mist, I reach out for your hand,
But you never grasped the value, the cost

You remained oblivious, indifferent,
To what truly mattered, you moved on,
In this space, you were never truly mine,
For here, I realize, you never belonged

YEARNING FOR THE CELESTIAL

The reality hit me hard again
Showed me, I don't belong to this world
I don't belong to anyone
I'm celestial
I have to shine above
Land sucks me inside it
I belong in the sky
Afar from adversities
From worldly expectations
The joys here are temporary
But scars are deep-rooted and permanent
And healing takes a lifetime
I belong to the universe
Let it consume every single particle of me
Let my soul rise from the body
Shining bright at night
Making the little child smile seeing me
Naming me and talking to me
Let my exhausted soul be valuable above

I'm just a dust particle on ground
Either ignored or wiped off
I'm celestial
Let me be in my place
Resting peacefully

WHERE IS MY PLACE?

Do I dwell in the past, present, or future?
Or am I lost in a different time's embrace?
Do I belong to those I hold dear?
Or am I merely a passerby here?

Do I reside within this beating heart?
Or is it just a vessel, set apart?
Do I fit into this earthly realm?
Or do I wander in an alternate realm?

Do I belong to another's embrace?
Or am I bound by empty space?
Where is my place in this world's song?
Where, oh where, do I truly belong?

FRACTURED RESOLVE

On that serene day, she came to grasp the extent of her shattered world

The emotions she once found simple to abandon

Now weighed heavily upon her,

Despite her previous determination to depart,

Furious, wounded, and resolute

She cannot fathom why, but something within her fractures,

Making departure a daunting task

She had believed herself prepared, or perhaps merely feigned readiness,

Yet now it churns her stomach

Maybe she wasn't prepared to confront the blows,

The ones she believed she had already weathered

AWAKENING THE WRITER WITHIN

Today, I awaken the writer within,

For who else can weave my thoughts into words?

Who else can turn heartbeats into verse,

And capture the essence of this little girl's excitement?

Who understands the way I perceive the world,

And what makes me growl or recoil?

Who comprehends my visions of rainbows and unicorns,

Yet also sees the reality of flowers and their thorns?

Let me awaken you, my friend!

Together, let's release what weighs heavy inside,

Allowing me to either bleed or shine

SILENT REVERBERATIONS

On some days, I might shut down myself
Only to revive me, a silent plea,
Much I've failed, stumbled in the dark,
Much I've lost, the scars left their mark
Much just went in vain, echoes remain,
They say, "time heals," but does it mend?
All I feel is numbness, a void inside,
A vacant space where emotions hide

Much noise, yet not much joy,
Much unrest, not much blessed,
A world full of illusions, mirages in disguise,
Where truth is obscured, behind veils of lies
But amidst the chaos, a glimmer of hope,
A flicker of light, in the vast scope
For even in darkness, there's a chance to find,
A path to peace, a tranquil mind

MIRAGE

Your love resembles a mirage's guise,
Distant yet alluring to searching eyes
As I draw near, its truth belies,
An illusion veiled in love's disguise

Your love, a fleeting illusion, fades from view
We stand apart, no bond to construe,
No belongingness between me and you

YOUR SWEET ALBATROSS!

On a love ship, you sailed afar
In the middle of the sea with shores apart;
You, the titular mariner, hungry and thirsty
Sailing towards a destination in adversity;
Looking up in the sky, waiting for a sign
You know you are running out of time;
Helpless, holding your cross
To save you, here I come, your Albatross!

You see me with gloomy eyes
Fellow seafarers have a reason to rejoice;
As luck for them, here I arise
You don't believe, it's all lies
In the wide-open sky, for my love I fly;
You held your crossbow to shoot
I fall on the deck, sighed last and hoot;
They believe, it's an omen you have come across
Here I die, your sweet Albatross!

They knew it's the beginning of an end
You don't know how virtues can mend;
The deed was performed already
As you stand in the lost sea with vanity
But they believe, you've lost your sanity;
You're a destroyer, you lost love, they curse,
As retribution, they hung me around your neck
Till you die, I rested on your chest, your sweet Albatross!

A DAY OF LIBERATION

She set herself free for a day,
Danced and screamed without delay
Living in the moment, worries shed,
Embracing joy instead
For just one day, she dared to be,
Free from constraints, wild and free

TRANSIENT BLOSSOMS

You were my moonflower, I see you rise

I spent hours, days, weeks, and months nurturing you;

And you outshined my garden with your presence

You remained there for a while till you find another world;

It brightened my days and crumbled to rest

I still think if my efforts to grow you over me were worthy;

The answer is I saw the beautiful you and I see you fade

Maybe that was our relationship- short and sweet,

You were my moonflower, I see you die

SHATTERED TRUST

In the deep sea, her ship once sailed,
Repaired by him, love never failed
But wrecked again, into pieces torn,
She dived alone, her spirit worn

Emerging strong, from the sea's embrace,
She saw him standing, with a smirk on his face
She knew then, trust was a fragile thread,
In a world where hearts often bled

Through trials endured, she learned to see,
The strength within, to set her free
No longer reliant on a fleeting shore,
She charted her path, forevermore

In the wake of storms, she found her truth,
Resilient, brave, in the face of youth
For in the depths, she learned to strive,
No longer bound by love's cruel dive

UNANSWERED QUESTIONS

Do you ever think of me at dawn's light,
Or is it just my thoughts that take flight?

Does the absence of my voice cause you pain,
As it does to me, like a constant refrain?

Do you sense my presence in the air,
Or am I the only one who feels you there?

Do you imagine us wandering side by side,
As I do when I drive, lost in the ride?

Do our shared kisses and embraces fade,
In your memory, or are they all replayed?

Do you love me with the same intensity,
Or is it just a one-sided affinity?

RAINY REVERIE

In the rhythm of raindrops, she finds calmness,
Escaping reality, she enters a dreamscape's embrace
Seated in her cozy nook, a sanctuary of peace,
Watching droplets dance on the window, a gentle release

In one hand, an unread book awaits her gaze,
In the other, a cup of tea, a comforting craze
Outside, puddles fill, splashing in joyous delight,
As she savors the symphony of rain, a tranquil sight

Her mother's voice fills the air with 80's melodies,
Soothing tunes that carry her to distant reveries
Pets rest nearby on the carpet, serenaded by the rain,
In this moment, she knows, she has everything to gain

For in her heart, she holds her perfect place,
An oasis of calm, a haven of grace
Here, amidst the rain's gentle symphony,
She finds her fantasy, her sanctuary, her reverie

ROOTS OF ANGUISH

Last night, he visited in dreams anew,
Asked if I'm angry, tears in my view
Lips moved, yet silence claimed its due,
For yes, anger within me grew

Angry for absence in your life's domain,
For seeing you happy, causing inner pain
Angry for your choice, causing strife,
And anguished that you've moved on in life

Rooted deep within, this anger's grasp,
Transformed to pain, a burden to clasp
Removing it would take a part of me,
So let me dwell in this agony

Forever mourning what could have been,
Living without you, lost in the din
And though I wished you'd understand,
The weight of longing left unplanned

A SHOWER OF SOLACE

In the midday's relentless showers,
She cries out, her anguish devours
Water cascades from face to skin,
Her tears mingling, a cleansing spin

With soap's lather, she scrubs away,
The hurt that's haunted, day by day
Struggling hard to rid the dirt,
Of agony that's left her hurt

The pouring water, a soothing stream,
Calms her mind, a tranquil dream
As knocks echo upon the door,
She knows she's cleansed, her spirit sore

She lingers still, beneath the flow,
Wrapped in arms, her pain to know
Understanding her own despair,
In the solace of water's care

Eventually, she steps away,
Knowing peace is but a stay
Yet in this moment, she finds release,
Her muscles relaxed, her soul at peace

FREEDOM'S EMBRACE

I long to unclench these fists of mine,
Release the burdens I've carried in time
To find a place where prejudice fades,
And numbness no longer casts its shades

Free from thoughts that weigh me down,
Dragging my body, causing it to drown
From situations that deem me unworthy,
And burdens that make my back feel sturdy

Free from opinions, suggestions unkind,
That clutter my mind, clouding my find
From every empty cell, sick within,
And fears that haunt, beneath my skin

Then, in this freedom, I'll truly thrive,
No longer just breathing, but alive
A life untethered, unbound, and free,
In this newfound freedom, I'll truly be

FLIGHT OF RESILIENCE

I apprehend my life sometimes,
More than highs it has lows,
More than wishers, I've foes

On some days I'd given up, on some I survived,
Less appreciated and more ridiculed,
The more I wanted to detach, the more I was glued

Deceived many times, I'm still a believer,
I'm not a blender, I'm an eye-opener,
Don't pull me down, I'm not here to win any hearts,
I own wings, I don't want to crawl

ETERNAL DEVOTION

Since I'm in love
I'm in a trance,
The way love came to my heart
I only remember you, rest I forgot,
I should cast away the evil eye
I want you to be by my side

My love is like amber, since antiquity
Here and now and for eternity
In one soul we meet, you make me a deity

I'm smitten by you
I'm smitten by you

You're my drug, you make me high
Come let's kiss, let there be no sigh,
Put on some music, play with my hair
Clutch my hands and poof some air

Let my pulse fall and passion makes me speechless
Let me tremble in your arms,
Let the fire grow and love me no less,
Let me close my eyes before you leave
You make a deity, I believe

YOU WERE MY HERO

You were my hero,
Before I met you, I understood love,
But with you, I truly felt it,
In a short time, you gave abundantly,
And I've never felt so precious in my life

You were my hero,
In my past, I gave love,
Yet you showed me how to receive it,
Your care was immense,
And I've never felt so precious in my life

You were my hero,
I was always a supporting character,
But you empowered me to be the protagonist,
Your optimism was infectious,
And I've never felt so precious in my life

You were my hero,
I dreamt of fairy tales all my life,

Yet you shattered that illusion,
Leaving me to face reality alone,
And I've never felt so shattered in my life

DESERT BLOSSOM

In deserts and wastelands, she thrives,

'Neath the blazing sun and molten sands she survives

Tall she stands, amidst adversity's call;

Plump and prickly, yet undeniably pretty,

Tough and tenacious, in nature's gritty city

Tolerant, independent, her adaptability sure,

Wild and compatible, her spirit pure

Made of thorns, yet blossoms she showers,

Awaiting nature's rain, her strength empowers

Unmarred by trials, she stands, steadfast,

She is a cactus in a pot, a testament to resilience unsurpassed

AWAKENING

In the haze of cigarette smoke, I find solace,
My body sloshed, seeking respite from the race
Days blend into nights, as I lay still,
Trying to silence the clamor of my will

Bruised and battered, scars tell tales untold,
Yet it's the wounds within that truly take their hold
Unconscious pleas for sleep clash with waking strife,
As I lie awake, questioning the meaning of life

What have I done to myself in this despair?
Is losing myself worth someone who doesn't care?
But now, amidst the darkness, a glimmer I see,
It's time to mend, to rebuild, to set myself free

No longer will I lose myself in the night,
I'll gather the pieces and step into the light
For I refuse to let this pain define who I am,
It's time to reclaim my essence, piece by piece, I'll stand

So let the cigarettes fade, the bruises heal,
I'll embrace the journey, however long it may feel
For in the brokenness, I'll find strength anew,
And in rebuilding myself, I'll rediscover the true

A BITTERSWEET ECHO

In a tender embrace, she leaned on his shoulder,
His gentle touch, a soothing balm, he bestowed
Their eyes met, a silent exchange untold,
In that fleeting moment, a world they both hold

With a glance, they shared their deepest desires,
As they danced in the flames of passion's fires
A kiss, a seal upon their hearts, a vow,
Yet now, they yearn to erase, disavow

For what once was sweet, now a bitter truth,
A memory they long to shed, uncouth
Oh, to unlearn the echoes of that kiss,
To erase the memory, what bliss it is

But time, relentless, etches each line,
In the fabric of memory, it entwines
Though they strive to forget, it lingers still,
A bittersweet echo, against their will

FRAGMENTS OF SORROW

Sitting on a broken chair, heart torn apart,
Watching it decay, a silent work of art;
It waited patiently, for your return,
You arrived nonchalant, its anguish you spurn
Hoping for a glimmer, a guiding light,
But you shattered it further, deepening the plight
Your abandonment cuts, a cruel shard,
It weeps with every scar, deeply marred
Broken into shards, abandoned in despair,
It embraces darkness, with a silent prayer

NOT SO DEPARTED LOVE

In the quiet corners of my soul,
Where echoes of love once found a home,
I thought I severed ties, let go,
Yet in shadows, your presence still roams

I turned away, shut tight the door,
When your words cut deep, wounded core,
But why, oh why, does my heart implore,
For a love, I thought I'd lost before?

Each step I took, a path apart,
From the pain you etched upon my heart,
Yet in dreams, you still impart,
A haunting melody, refusing to depart

Though distance grew, and silence reigned,
I find you lingering, unexplained,
In every thought, you still remain,
A ghost of love, refusing to wane

A DANCE OF TRUTH

In the profundity of trust, we lose our sight,
To a world imagined, where dreams take flight
But in this reverie, we neglect the cost,
For what's real slips away, irretrievably lost

In the embrace of illusion, we find solace sweet,
Yet reality whispers, a truth hard to meet
For the bubble of imagination, so fragile and fair,
Will burst asunder, leaving us bare

In the realm of dreams, all seems sublime,
But reality's grip, withstands the test of time
For what's real is ours, in its stark clarity,
While imagination fades, into obscurity

So heed the call of truth, let fantasies wane,
For in the end, it's reality we gain
In the dance between what's imagined and true,
Remember, it's the real that sees us through

NATURE'S LAP

In mountains tall, where deodars sway,
Green earth below, blue skies display
With teacup held, eyes filled with grace,
Soul finds peace in this tranquil space

Not more, nor less, but perfect, see,
A moment's bliss, serenely free
Comfortable, content, in this sweet embrace,
In nature's arms, find solace and grace

O' MY FRAGILE HEART

My heart so fragile
Shattered and stumbled upon a million times
Frozen, sealed, and put together again
Living a lifeless life
After love has gone away
It barely knew how to beat
I, no longer carried warmth
All I knew what pain is
You stepped in my life with a promise to caress it forever
You concealed my heart with love
My heart bloomed again
After long faded laughter
You fixed that smile again
You stayed there for a while
Let our love grow
With your sparkling eyes and magic touch
You made me believe in miracles
From quiet sighs and disrupted breaths
I was breathing freely

Just when we mend things
You chose to leave
You held my heart in your hands
It made a creaking sound
Yet broken in pieces again
O' my heart so fragile

UNBREAKABLE WINGS

In the grand theatre of existence, she dances to the rhythm of struggle, a relentless waltz from the moment of her first breath. Born amidst the tumult of life's entry, she fought to stake her place in a world teeming with challenges. Racing against the current of societal expectations, she sought not just to compete but to triumph, her footsteps echoing with determination.

In the fabric of her voyage, love emerged as both a beacon and a battleground, a quest fraught with the complexities of the heart. Each stride forward, each embrace of vulnerability, was met with the harsh scrutiny of judgment, her very essence dissected under the unforgiving gaze of others.

Her existence, a kaleidoscope of struggles, became a canvas upon which society projected its biases and preconceptions. Every facet of her being, from her thoughts to her appearance, was weighed and measured against a flawed and skewed standard.

Yet amidst the cacophony of voices clamoring for her conformity, she remained steadfast in her resilience. For she knew that strength was not measured by the absence of struggle, but by the courage to endure, to rise time and time again in the face of adversity.

To those who would underestimate her, who would diminish her worth with their narrow-mindedness, she offered a silent defiance. For she was not bound by the limitations of their perceptions, but soared beyond them, a phoenix reborn from the ashes of their ignorance.

She needed no validation, no affirmation of her worth, for within her beat the heart of a warrior, a force to be reckoned with. To all the superheroes who graced her life, who stood as beacons of inspiration and resilience, she offered a simple yet profound message: love and respect.

THE FAULT IN MY STARS

In the serenity of a mundane day,
I met your gaze, a gentle sway
No grandeur in sight, just plain and true,
Yet in your eyes, a world I knew

A simple boy, with darkness deep,
Admiration gleamed, secrets to keep
In that moment, a bond unfurled,
A love so pure, it shook my world

A spark ignited, a flame did grow,
From that hour, a love did flow
Piece by piece, my heart you stole,
Until it was yours, a treasure whole

But time, unkind, it took its toll,
And love's bright flame began to dull
The fire once fierce, now faded, gone,
Leaving me to wonder what went wrong

Yet still I carry, in memories deep,
The love we shared, the dreams we'd keep
Though love may die, the soul survives,
In memories, where our love thrives

So I'll tend to these memories, day by day,
Not to bind the roots, but to find my way
For in their waters, my soul finds peace,
In the echoes of love that will never cease

LOST AND FOUND

In a world where hearts are tossed aside like forgotten treasures, hers was flung into the abyss of a lost and found box. Abandoned by the one who once held it dear, it was discovered anew by another soul, who painstakingly pieced it back together and nurtured it until it beat with love once more. But just as her heart began to swell with affection, he chose to cast it aside yet again, leaving it to wither in the confines of the box. Mocked and toyed with by indifferent hands, her heart bore the scars of neglect and betrayal.

Yet, she refused to let despair consume her. With tender care, she tended to her wounded heart, allowing it to bleed out the pain until every drop was shed. And in the gentle embrace of self-love, she nurtured her mended heart, allowing it to flourish once more, to thrive, to bask in its own resilience and beauty.

I AM NOBODY'S POETRY

Silent abyss of solitude, I roam,
My verses dance, but find no dome
In the whispers of the night, I yearn,
For my soul's echo, yet to discern

Each line penned with tender grace,
A longing heart, a sacred space
Yet, in the vast expanse, I stray,
A poet's plight, day by day

Unfurling dreams upon the page,
An endless quest, a timeless stage
But still, I linger in obscurity,
A poet's fate, a silent plea

So let me wander, let me be,
In the vast expanse, wild and free
For though I am nobody's poetry,
In my words, I find eternity

SWINGS WERE COOL

The playground filled with joy,
A little girl, a little boy,
Their eyes alight with wonder bright,
As they explore the world in flight

With giggles bubbling, they run free,
Through meadows green, beneath the tree,
Their laughter dances in the air,
As they chase dreams without a care

But what captures their hearts, you see,
Is not the slide or climbing tree,
It's the simple joy that swings provide,
As they sway together side by side

With tiny hands gripping tight,
They soar through the golden light,
Their smiles wide, their hearts ignite,
In this moment, everything feels right

For in the rhythm of their play,
They find a moment to stay,
In innocence, pure and true,
Where every dream feels within view

So let them swing, let them play,
In the magic of childhood's sway,
For in the innocence they find,
A world of wonder, endlessly kind

THE GAZE

In the veiled sanctuary of gazes, we entrust our unspoken truths, those narratives you decipher with a graceful touch. You navigate the labyrinth of emotions, reading between the lines of unspoken confessions, offering solace in the language of understanding. Within these eyes, where love has yet to find its foothold, you unearth hidden beauty, declaring them as radiant beacons in the darkness of the soul.

With each glance, you unravel the intricacies of sorrow, delving deep into the mysteries concealed beneath layers of kohl. These eyes, adorned with secrets, yearn to confide in your empathetic gaze. Yet, you recognize that words often fall short in expressing the depth of pain, and so you weave a tapestry of joy, shielding these eyes from the sting of tears.

Who are you, with your intuitive wisdom and compassionate heart? How do you navigate the labyrinth of emotions with such grace?
Your ability to discern the unspoken whispers of the soul is a testament to your profound insight.
In the silent exchange of glances, you find solace, understanding, and love, transcending the limitations of language and speaking directly to the heart.

www.ingramcontent.com/pod-product-compliance
Lightning Source LLC
LaVergne TN
LVHW041234150826
845673LV00008B/2382

* 9 7 9 8 8 9 3 6 3 3 9 0 0 *